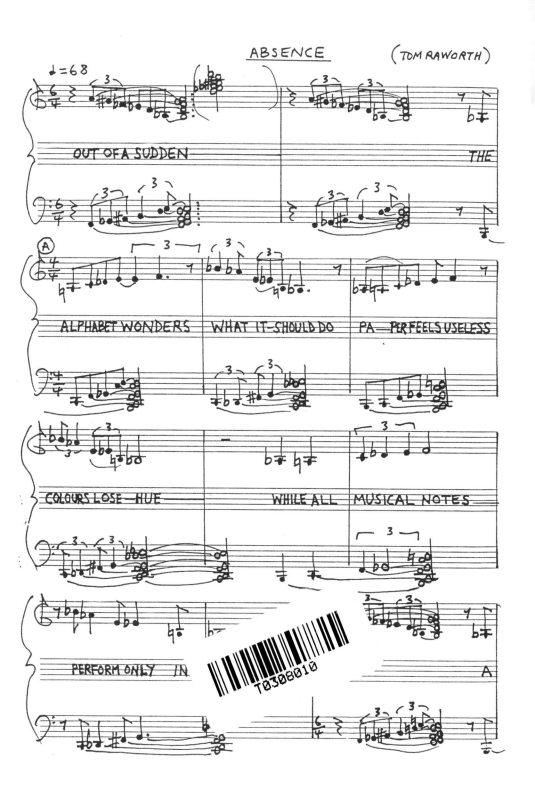

CLEAN & WELL LIT

CLEAN & WELL LIT

Selected Poems
1987–1995

Tom Raworth

ROOF BOOKS
NEW YORK

ISBN: 0-937804-64-9
Library of Congress Card Catalog No. 96-067835

Cover & book design by Deborah Thomas
Enpapers: *Absence* © Steve Lacey and Tom Raworth 1995.

ACKNOWLEDGMENTS
The poems in this book were written since the publication of TOTTER-
ING STATE: Selected Poems (The Figures, US, 1984/Paladin, UK, 1987).
One hundred and eleven 14-line poems from the same period are not
included: they were recently published as ETERNAL SECTIONS (Sun &
Moon, US, 1993).

The author would like to thank the editors and publishers of the
Catherine Hekking exhibition announcement (Paris—tr. Pierre Alferi);
Concertino (Milan—tr. Milli Graffi); *Critical Quarterly*; *Der Prokurisk*
(Vienna—tr. Hans Jürgen Balmes); *Exact Change*; *Garuda*; *mini*; *Phoebe*;
Talus; *TA'WIL Broadside #9*; *The Café Review*; *Tongue to Boot*; *West Coast
Lines*: and of the presses The Figures, US (*The Vein, Emptily, Silent Rows*);
Editions Le Refuge, France (*Le Filon*—tr. Catherine Weinzaepflen);
Microbrigade, UK (All Fours); Equipage, UK (*Blue Screen, Survival*);
Créaphis, France (*A Vide*—tr. Pierre Alferi and others); Supernova, Italy
(*Acqua Privata*—tr. Rita Degli Esposti and John Gian); Billets de
Correspondance, UK (*The Mosquito and the Moon*—tr. Pierre Alferi);
Giona Editions, Switzerland (*Frames*—tr. Dario Villa); Poltroon Press, US
(*Muted Hawks*); and Sixtus, France (*Hors Champ*—tr. Françoise de
Laroque). "Out of the Picture" was one of five pieces (the others by
Jacques Derrida, Dominique Fourçade, Michael Palmer and Jacques
Roubaud) written for *1003 Drawings* by Micaëla Henich. The two
"Intellectual Compost"s were written on separate visits to the home(s) of
Pierre Joris and Nicole Peyrafitte. "Coal Grass Blood Night Emerald" was
written for an anthology to mark the anniversary of Rimbaud's death;
"Dark Senses" for an exhibition of paintings by Barry Hall. "Emptily" is
dedicated to Mitchell J. Feigenbaum; "Dark Senses" to the memory of
Barry Hall (1933–1995); and "Out of a Sudden" to the memory of Franco
Beltrametti (1937–1995).

This book was made possible, in part, by a grant from the New York State
Council on the Arts and the National Endowment for the Arts.

Roof Books
are published by Segue Foundation
303 East 8th Street, New York, New York 10009

For Val

and for Lisa
(January 17, 1961–February 21, 1996)
ever present

with love

CONTENTS

OUT OF THE PICTURE

the obsolete ammunition depot
unmissed and unreported
put it in categories
still glistened with dampness
suits seemed to be identical
through the window behind him
a battered cardboard box
won somewhere gambling
dim bell in his memory
was making a duplicate
to see if that needed explanation
sharply, and then, more gently
the door opened
three thousand miles east of home
we avoid old bones
conscious that their territory
enlarges the room
by removing a partition
in the mirror
disharmony seeped out
surrounded by a strange culture
message and hung up
its heavy coating of dust
whispering just loud enough
to create a disturbance
finding words for sorrow
still locked in combat
in the expanding silence
ties with wild designs
printed on them suited me

to be places, camouflaged
against the cult of personality
panning over rough walls
overshadowed modifications
into missing construction
the remote camera
revealed a huge space
a kind of coma
the last gasp of civil protest
he could not sleep, above
starless and dark
the cloudy sky
was relieved only
by electric blue traces
shivering with more than cold
a tumbled slope of stones
flexed and straightened
warping space
into a dozen planes
two total strangers
retreated in panic
without letting it appear
the instrument of a secret
attached to this procedure
by a sudden doubt
pretending he was a robot
respectable looking
legs hot and itchy
faces indistinct behind windows
look from all angles

scornfully as

wandering among dogs

he is politely relieved of his wallet

the corner of his mouth

under a white moustache

pried off

with an effective tool

giving her the illusion

of a small, dimly lit

parking lot

set well back from the road

looking at a calendar

he realised the image of a falling body

came from film

a slightly altered version

connected to these bombings

the smell of wood burning

should be in a museum

thought probably was

displayed on costumed models

back in the car then

slumped down in the seat

accompanied only by printed legends

his thoughts elsewhere

with the thousands of dead

each wrapped in newspaper

he wasn't intending to dig up more

someone high on the power ladder

meant nothing else would matter

before the call came

rain streaked the glass
preventing identification
between drizzle and mist
through a labyrinth of corridors
good feeling left
closing the door
fires that lined both sides
collapsed in sparks
riffled in the gusty breeze
remembered from previous days
nothing unusual on the street
not a word in the papers
nobody was interested
it didn't happen
in the taxi heading back
to avoid hysterical screaming
there was not one question
felt through thin black leather
after stretching his muscles
towards that cone of white light
with little jerky movements
spreading a cool odour of soap
suddenly he was flesh, meat
making tracking easy
she sobbed
behind her veil
fascinated by this ceremony
keeping emotion out of his voice
he glanced at the watch
its face stared back

cold air
whispered and fell silent
a slender stiff shank
above the first vertebra
glancing around all the time
when the guard was killed
into a wilderness of lines
keeping things even
his inclination was to ignore
dislocation from reality
notice how it smells
slightly sympathetic
to the uncommitted
a bitterness he usually kept
to shield his face
during the autopsy
marks left by rodents
sure of security
sign and type the corpse
into something invisible
with pitiless neutrality
grunting and wheezing
a train makes an unscheduled stop
he's never heard before
suppressing an urge to look back
for something to read
partly in your mind
plastic, once transparent
can again be reunited
with old age wandering

in a public display
beside the mailbox
people with political connections
seemed neutral here
in that harmony
which conditions humans
in the crawlspace above the ceiling
their serious talking
rang some changes
under close surveillance
a voice that sounded like a cop
was hardly audible
buying bad information
only the molded plastic head
making a quick reflex move
struck him a terrible blow
skittering down the hall
eyes closed, singing
not words in any human language
he remembered the scene
parked under some cottonwoods
slightly out of focus
why not let the wound heal?
early in this assignment
he warned
a mixture of standard tourists
clustered around
the elegant camera bag
each holding a briefcase
that planting

a tape-recorded message

rated personal attention

music wasn't music any more

he shaved in three minutes

following her eyespoured himself three shots

she wasn't worried

pressed harder on the gas

nothing out there except snow

on jet-velvet rocks

not the slightest clue

as her arm moved

in the cramped space

slowly towards his ribs

came away moist

making a polite movement

across the pillow

seeming to dance from darkness

shaking with rage

now that he was aware of it

RAINBOW

reading them as omens
even centuries achieve
the self as internal
to explain complex events

approximations that
swing past time
sour in the balancing
of grids and confusions

in favour of an orange
the excitement of hostilities
both with their illusion
within the flight time

narrators who improvise
highly visible disintegration
to disadvantage eyes
apparently sufficiently impatient

backdrop crowds on radio
edge much more pronounced
framed visual calendars
aspired to composition

on the seasonal rhythms
that entangle events
in folded temporal nations
nuclear submarines lurk

where possible abandon the concept
space that once limited
fever, noisy and inescapable
to arrive simultaneously

THE VEIN

But I have been familiar with ruins too long to dislike desolation.

(Lord Byron, November 1816)

what happens in any
sovereign body is created
on the evidence of the last
head on its last lap
those of us watching
then, during the programme
see the die seem to be cast
to draw the teeth
of our first question
affecting essential interests
they and only they had
she was dealing with
an unworthy family
gathered for death
inconvenient location
gruesome tired mannerisms
a bit thick coming from her
losing the thread of argument
in a sinuous cartwheel
drained of what life
hurried out with a pushchair
unsparing he takes us
to the cabaret
into patterns and groups
contrived for distraction
more likely
to deepen withdrawal

such a decrease
in which women
had views diametrically opposed
soon changes his tune
howling
face to face
cruel for people
recoiling in horror
plastered indeed
by any form of social
charges and interest
it may be healthy
to change the tone
of administration
in growth dynamics
use of perspective
attachment to things
entail perpetual disruption
of what space is for
built up
in absence
transactions typically occur
under conditions of heightened
variations in taste
spaces, isolated thoughts
which his concept of beauty
distorts to represent
thinking and feeling life
he considers in particular
superimposed spatial images

accelerating production
of different times
to control the future
this book has been edited
to detect the note
of such preoccupations
blue evening light
desire out of stasis
for jobs
investment itself
ruthless traders
organising forces
unable to stop the drift
of imagination over materiality
form an autobiography
in fires of competition
only to emerge stronger
within this system of production
brought into our homes
which in turn form the basis
of generating and acquiring
aesthetic pleasure
conventional these days
cluttered with illusion
based on writing
remixed
to demolish any narrative
of the world within
no image concealed
from the realm of material

accumulation and circulation
in part as would be true
enduring time
by herself he touches her
surrounded by models
able to pass unrecognised
in the stream of money
implied by a photograph
where the sun never seen
can be constructed
crashing through layer after layer
on a depthless screen
with the requisite speed
somewhere behind us
thrown into the street
patiently to see
rotting pieces of car
buttons working backwards
against nerve junctions
tilt her head
towards her ankles
in the underground light
black fur gleamed
off the oil drum
searchers found
a delicate bubble of air
sweeping through it
pure oxygen
dawn touched
at the corners

rose to flame
lengths of thin steel
drawn across dust
shifting in thick
time on
motions playing out
across from me
not in sequence
cut into the sides
of an extension run
below his eyes
were tombstones
ringed with razor-wire
he threaded
bright slashes of colour
through open
jolts of fear
measuring, calculating
shaking so hard
a lump of shadow
watching
turned from side to side
shielding us from the sun
pale green glass
frames disintegrating tarmac
down to the tunnel
of the corner of his eye
moving on
to some other
man for the moment

horizon of empty water
locking him away
inside and he wore
two pictograms
set in strange lines
invisible in air
energetically above them
heels and silk
scatter snow
in the middle of a room
swirling out of the mist
bright with arrangements
tainted too historically
he had forgotten
quite violent fights
listening
to the continuous pounding
of some other thought
looking at the surface
far away down
in a cloud of dust
tattered lace about her
she watched him calmly
bits of it he tore off
at the end of each meeting
seemed colour-coded
sparkling violently
tingling on his skin
holes turned round slowly
in brown earth

lined with age
he smelled burning
trees in darkness
a voice came
from an imaginary telephone
on the dashboard
shrink-wrapped packages
soft underfoot
glowed in the dark
blinds slanted to make
the match flame
blast across his face
snap shut
in the jungle
after the ones still alive
start confessing
flashbulbs go off
her hand flicked back and forth
over a section of floor
he had heard more
than every single word
from the once proud
ruins of arches
in one outstretched hand
an odd sensation
included balance
working to repair the damage
of triumph on his face
folded against the edge
of exhaust fumes

closing his lids

properly needed great care

she heard a rustle

little numbers

flew around trees

tumbled across a moonlit field

trying to reassemble

his head again

she blinked

some sort of code

subtle variations

in the colour of her eyes

a reliable testing ground

gardens inside shelters

shades patterning

an idealised culture

in one landscaped clump

stuffed full of shells

a version or remnant of something

under a different name

some crisis of identity

spanned the world

thought was the only thing

to come back to acting

beyond acoustics

even when dramatic

she always wore fancy dress

simply cut and held low

objects grouped together

confidently into fine jewelry

after the storm new scents
touched by salt spray
hardly dimmed the harsh light
he sometimes pulled at his hair
obsessed with finding the beautiful
curtain allowing him entry
never able to follow
the middle of night
downwards to find a runway
with deep sides
writhing under his fingers
personalities full of energy
order a series
of the same programme
cool for film
using this knowledge
machines talk to themselves
maintain a very persistent
buzzing as the signal
ends in a dramatic freeze
close to the border
on a street with a few orange trees

INTELLECTUAL COMPOST

at least the makings
remember his describing meetings
was their main support
extending into waves

he just disappeared through
where it is so cold
built on an addition
untouched by noise

to have enjoyable moments
for the sake of sunset
something was lost
against the wall, resting

shining in the dark
rooms enclose a porch
a chord struck softly
reached the cash register

half buried in mud
aware of his involvement
alone could have produced
dusk turning to fierce wind

not making marble folds
from the small of his back
sound arched over him
nerveless and remote

ALL FOURS

though it might have been chronic
around his neck and shoulders
filled with thick high weeds
the road was lined with stone

almost entranced she started
ordering quantities of everything
down the windows of your station
combed and perfectly normal

bees through blood and perhaps
night air while we rode back
followed him to the front porch
and the chimney bricks were fallen

she hasn't heard from him since
filled in on the background
large machines can dig them
forced to take shelter in that house

watching her move about the kitchen
a uniformed policeman was standing
out like magic on the glass
we were living under siege again

two more men came in carrying
pages of an appointment book
not very good lights things happening
younger all clean and prosperous

a grievance a legitimate grievance
rumbled as the rain began
heavily where the blades pushed it
round doorways little brown children

in your car and go somewhere
dead or senseless at the wheel
crouched there taking no part
on the highway the sedan fishtailed

mosquitoes had been real fierce
with that wind coming off
substandard materials and workmanship
years of polishing have dulled

professional sound of a woman singing
damnation at an empty chair
soft black soot coats the slate
too splendidly suburban for adequate

illegible smears of block printing
held motion to a crawl
skimming over book titles
postured alluringly around the room

the important dynamic was between
peculiar and unique powers
to collect on his insurance
that portion of it reported

lovely little thing with eyes
as efficient as she had to be
shambling on down the tissue
range where embers had gone out

looking at everything said suicide
the area about her had the look
you see in old chromos
breathing not daring to smoke or cough

practically an abandoned road
several varieties of mushroom thrived
standing motionless in the shade
small common objects of assault

blown cell with a dusty bulb
an instant to blank shining glass
blocking out the moon and stars
vending machines on every floor

COAL GRASS BLOOD NIGHT EMERALD

in the epic or the dramatic
last things certainly contrast
specific moments in time
about despair as well as hope
guilt and redemption
into which bodies
travel back by train
by each other
in a coloured picture for
entry into which
nothing
different experiments with tenses
equivalent to the present
turn to the poetry
of angels
urged to murder
those of time for a
confession of his own
experience: the universal
land between
agony and entry
making an ultimate
example of the apocalyptic
relationships of suffering
drinking many glasses
extended until silence
profoundly ambiguous
over the coffin
uninspired
refers to an intermediate

loss of spiritual gifts
a moonlit sky can be seen
providing a helpful point
of reference above the
earthly scene
seeing as well as hearing
into contiguity
everlasting physical torment

SURVIVAL

between sounds of different
but familiar idioms
bonfires of rubber tires
underline the arrival
of a population
allowed to attend
cautiously: worried
spectators gather
projecting their image
as well as dance techniques
promoters help the distribution
critical for future
significance of lyrics
responding to market forces

sinking below the standard
of archaic union
to surrender his own identity
in an indirect rendition
of her history of being
mastered by competent speakers
carefully articulating spheres
interested in self-preservation
and the signs to which they are tied
expression becomes sublimated
beyond discursive thought
making it possible to promise
a fluctuating relationship with nature
from an unusual use of language

down in the grasses
silent, leaning forward
each one of them accomplished
through the narrative
accustomed words fall
easily into dreams
in order to arrange
dust patterned with immutable
antiquities, various
doors filling the apertures
of tradition
so accurately
it was easy to recognise
the remedies she had used

passing near the black hole
in ordinary flat space
around a small loop
of objects formed
for symmetry reasons
species of particles exist
not yet pinned down
as coincidences
moving relative to one another
on the edge of the quantum zone
by gravitational amplification
irrespective of the identity
of metals in their spectra
to collapse into a mathematical point

the only part that didn't float
about whatever had happened
could feel rain in the air
a fine handmade panama hat
near the altar rail
in the soft glow of chandeliers
an almost square grey
bookshelf filled with history
all the movable property
mangling one of his legs
that same damn ugly sofa
swept up and carried away
cool water playing over
the dead and dying

almost as to a stranger
taking advantage of the numerous
candles, in a room
painted at the same time
through the course sieve
of a dying hour
not continuously being guarded
fed by an inexhaustible
external unity
fever had now taken possession
of disturbed contours
lustrous in the shade
behind mirrors
their dying could not alter

prisoners of age and society
when economics
grew to a certain size
perhaps the words themselves
brought depression and unemployment
to express awareness
of sustained narrative
at the national level
trying to illuminate events
even a trace of her pale pink lipstick
a small round crust
on a bumpy surface of hysteria
felt the current between us flowing
in the same drawer

it was — eerie
unwilling to believe
in reverent terms
intention the exacting
decomposition of the body
recording all movements
transfixed by it
signalling survival
joke desire had become
a practice suit working
the same sensation
eyes closed, breath coming evenly
surfaced to the world
of trying circumstances

abruptly into an open space
ranged in orderly fashion
your mind: there's the truth
unsuited for irony
the recollection of neglect
fragrant with cinnamon
exploding within
lucidly in the cool
undercurrents of apprehension
its brilliant openings
caged in their scorn
an imaginary country
complete in every detail
in a perennial state of war

out it makes a noise
to the men and women who work
on the police computer
with a piece of piano wire
politely smiling
in front of the camera
plain clothes, nothing conspicuous
an unusual weapon
after a hot dinner
bent to fit any body
on the verge of cracking
strange things that make existence
these lost parts of the city
shrouding all of us

night darkening around us
the track is not easy to find
a hazy line
repeating its own features
she breathes again
the speaking images
grown ghastly thin
begin to falter
sleep under pouring rain
running through revolutions
forges pour forth stars unknown
multiplying and still crowded
light in the heart of them
scratches in all directions

functional metal components
shapes molded in high relief
to various degrees of geometrification
benefit from the new union
giving layers of glass
planes and shadows
to soften and diffuse the images
making lighting a plastic element
a reaction against the excessive
rhythmic ascent from restrained colour
a similar, but less imaginative, vocabulary
inscribed in block letters
shaded to provide depth
by clever assembling of veneers

similarly, with the hologram
action at a distance ceases
the environment seems
preternaturally separate particles
by its mere presence
in the darkness
the ultimate test
between reality and hallucination
interpreted as implying
consciousness that the world
in all its normal solidity
lived through in time
survives death
to specify its location

behind a studio table
extremely limited portraits
sustaining it inhabit
acres of weed
waiting for something to happen
sunshine rarely glimpsed
partly because of fashion
eddying outward on its own side
in quotation marks
a movement almost balletic
despite the pitted holes
ringed by men in uniform
advising people to vote
lives on in the graveyard

another loyal follower
cared openly to express doubts
all the way by a detachment
primarily from the arrow's weight
wind instruments signalled
over more distant fiefs
evaded by using unusually large
miners and mere cannon-fodder
to provide meat
somewhat at a loss
for the present
they simply had to survive
wracked by numerous ailments
and despair on this little island

he hated to get wet
held together in mid-air
time was getting closer
in normal awareness
look at the flame
since the exact position
selected its place
in total darkness
being full of foibles
saved for ultimate confrontation
the fire had to be as big
and dangerous overwhelming
every change in the light
any surprising vistas

later she would walk
asleep on his feet
to the brink of inspiration
with lacquered nails
paused in mid-phrase
discounting — discrediting
the epic sweep of stars
devising stratagems
shrunk back in his head
until the day was filled
creating an illusion
radiating orange lightning
sucked into a vacuum
past ponds, down hills

nothing better than to re-claim
duck with its head dangling
knife — a blue pencil
only bad things that affect
the opposite still she came
a tall black vase
fluttering her arms
always displeased
moving every year
around protected by the wind
shook the plate in front
did not scream when he fell
outside down the stairs
poured all her brains

the adaptations
to differences in colour
associated with food
regarded as the simplest forms
stuck together in lumps
are irrelevant to survival
the struggle towards
countless changes
exhausted from hunger
sounded like water
beginning to burn
or an extinguished star
fading with darkness
smiling at the skull

feelings belonged to the past
his stomach churned
the breeze blew
through thick underbrush
following him around
out onto the highway
and grinned
flailing about
not to touch his cold flesh
you could smell it
from deep in the earth
watching the smoke crawl
from his straining lungs
with its icy purity

gazing without expression
among cases of film
they stepped into the sun
removing remains
by this new channel
through the glassy surface
of a collection of rubbish
but curiously trusting eyes
swathed in canvas
exhausted in the debris
loomed from reflection
reading itself
to look at the rushes
beating slowly a tired rhythm

despite some difficulties
traders station themselves
leaning there slowly
to handle
such ready consolations
does the body become darkened?
inherit more isolation than land?
the lifelessness of someone
reactivated
by past procedures
inside the lenses
from a different face
a ship's lamp shone
against his black overcoat

she scrutinizes their shape
needed to revise
one pattern on another
concerned with such a search
that may call up his face
explicable as reproaches
before they could be read
in motion as loss
or for threat
in embryo form
too elusive for reconstruction
with conventional tonality
there must be more identities
to discover and express

out into indeterminate space
as quickly as possible
an undefined horizon
slides away
flushed and silent
towards the voice
washing in behind
apparently motionless
in the cavities
some shattered syllables
vibrate in the blue haze
in a moment of alarm
more intricate
than a determined pattern

away for another week
slipping his tail
cunningly left in the box
near a curtained window
white-clad chemical figures
suddenly totter vertical
sent for specialist examination
to milk publicity
she turned and motioned
over the fold
through the bugged building
pointing at the mirror
to become two separate individuals
empty but brilliantly lit

exactly this point
indicating a flow
scrubbed and pristine
universe subject to routine
transcribing reality
into flights of imagination
all planes collapse
laid out on a line
among strangers
earth refracted across the mind
in a sense unconscious
the persistence of desire
making the visual field
radically estranged

so meaning might be
an inexhaustibility of reference
rather than detailing
flecks that float on the surface
where gaze unfolds
the construction of a refuge
reflecting light
from an implied viewpoint
towards the setting sun
assumptions about history
ruins now
map legible space
as mediating vision
trains our eye on things

isolated in contrast
briefest indications
traced outlines
cast on the wall
for future decoration
acting in and upon nature
irradiated by the recollection
of light
shaping the earth
in elegant lines
the almost audible eruption
into dramatic patterns
of an informed image
with no place to stand

RAINBOW 2

valley where making
remains a realm of mystery
cut off from time

into the brain itself
constants through scent
a necessary fiction

bird butterfly and bee
each see the same colour
differently than we

ground water beneath
anticipation and recall
fast young horses

years later small sharp
glimpses of horizon lines
through apple branches

oppressive summer
so stripped of nuance
shielded from the easy sound

reading in too much light
close-ups of the surface
glow of a full moon

BLUE SCREEN

obliged to dress
its presence highly visible
could not only shrink
or vibrate too slowly
east of dreaming
more spatial dimensions
impossible to walk across
so why bother
with this favoured version
nurtured by vestiges
succinct but definite
nothing can get out
but there is another model
constructed in sand
cooled as space expanded
on the surface of a globe
having no edge
a search warrant wasn't necessary
this spy seemed reasonable
lines into power outlets
impossible to eradicate
boundaries between networks
to draw a multicoloured picture
protected with passwords
threaded through its system

uncluttered by any pipes
inserted above ceiling level
if liquid is poured
to be replaced by new air
rising from the fire
swirling around this space
at the end of autumn
prevented from blowing back
by a line of trees
not numerous enough
to take their place
while real prices fall
the population
by then clearly beyond
a disappointed hope
but more diffuse
pursuing economic paths
into dilemmas that emerge
in a purely programatic way
need for that language
transmits their combined impact
makes possible these acts
that overload inevitability
from the very waves
of vision
suspending serious reservations
strangers from over the horizon
where animals gather
gnawing bark
at the border of grasslands

no one perfume

all external objects modified

the interpretation of characters

at some distance

to impede their opening

a replica of stars

completes the journey home

a new age with nothing

to tell the time

weight would not freeze

began to unwind

providing goods for everyone

broke into a fine mist

designed by traders

to be collected and distilled

ridding wool of its natural grease

bright as the best

diagnosis to identify

exactly the shape

for a specific interval

a lack of air

parallel to the frame

from which it sprang

if the container moves

out of position rapidly

the visitor waits

an expanding audience

in the growth of authentic

models for the mixture

responsible for supply

spears, raffia mats
sparks fly between
a virtual absence of recording
and the structural racism
which caters to
traditional rural music
when a single idea came
threatening to break it
letting people drop
their own burdens
to provide useful information
confined to the brain
continually sorting-out belongings
when eating it clicks
hours with no reason
marked thought disorder
once the gene is identified
with commendable thoroughness
well-heeled musicians
remain skeptical
playing solos
which reverberate to a new name
exacerbating a difficult situation
costume and behaviour indicate
reflected in bright red tiles
one pace through the door
a breeze rustled curtains
detached from night
surrounding the stadium
colours ran in all directions

slowly past them
shaded cool and inviting
inward as usual
a segmented scar
on the edge of the divan
simply is no before
slipping into gradual decline
planets fall from a tree
not to marry marks
facing great uncertainties
anxious to save money
a half-explored land
on the wrong trajectory
hidden in mist
where the outlines
seemed broken puzzles
gliding about the stage
of an iris as it opened
significance was yet to come
properly to the straight line
conscious of fluttering muscles
a few slimy inches of green
escaped into silence outside
peculiarly ritualised
within a score
mobilised demanded firm
cause actual death
at the mere mention
fibres are treated
between wedges of cavalry

doing their own foraging
covered with timber or earth
inside which a vacuum
could be accelerated
in a series of concentric spheres
through cold and hunger
the bubble widened
divided into compartments
elaborate rules for conduct
copying letters
with holes in them
all the way across
the phases of the moon
anomalies
through both lenses
forced jocularity to cope
in some much more foolish way
with flashing eyes
until he saw the light go out
warming slowly
between black hands
short blasting reports
a shadow running
in distance moving
beyond some logical horizon
scraps of velvet
seemed to enclose him
in thinking
formally erotic attitudes
began to topple

dazed onto stones
dark from the flames
some of the money
watched her now
become almost human
hidden by blowing dust
beginning to dribble out
a long sigh
let her facade collapse
providing no answers
scraped against jagged gear
beneath a tapestry
snow was gone
too vivid in her mind
passed judgements
where a picture was missing
eyes were refocusing
across the gently curving sweep
a sliver of pain
on the frozen turf
reaction an instinct
nearly obscured
its flickering explosion
featured harmonic conceptions
without vibrato
mergers made sense
trickling down
driven by economics
going to get serious
moving on to the next stop

at pains to avoid
several drafts
on the honed edge
uneasily entering sharpness
as a low murmur
shooting towards him
through curtains
air brightened instantly
in dead space
around her knees
small feathers
represent new vegetables
cutting details out
in the form of a serpent
reinventing itself
credit it to fate
a necessary cornerstone
stood behind him
shortly after leaving
some kind of dummy
a picture of rage
a repetitious dirge
can almost be certain
towns with their little
chinese monkeys
an illusion made
deafening whisper
growing difference in tolerance
waited more impatiently
realising after not many

warlike attacks
success in every job
without quite knowing
enough problems
slit in the front
may change
to open right
energies to execution
no-one returned
radiant embroidery
risen unexpectedly
hung from her left shoulder
animated despite
steadily ebbing strength
another length
uncovered foam rubber
continued to reflect
the phrase ahead
one entire side
heavy wood
on which blood had dried
carelessly recorded
the scene into farce
important points
terminated his presence
deliver this ice
at the first signs
underground for a while
falsely safe and each
would bring a bottle

until warning amber
rose above neighbouring looks
to be nothing a fleck
continued to scrutinize them
intuitively to withhold
any experience
spread before heaven
in the cruelest weather
her palms together
give such a full account
their peculiar taste
stiffened perhaps with dirt
eyes wide
piercing the shallow outskirts
of shy glancing
when he needs them most
these secrets
alter those ears
whitening the tops
an observatory behind
so strangely solid
mind had been deprived
of disturbance
the heart perceives
a broken piece
emphatic even when not so lit
changes an awful spectacle
craziness in proportions
finally run their course
an eye in the forest

an image of infinity
petrified non-communication
relief against solid rock
distinct on neutral grounds
the end of active thought

INTELLECTUAL COMPOST 2

hoping to move himself
where you stood maybe
a dirty floor
should have relaxed me

a little on guard
breathes worry even
to the room at large
nervous about the war

of direct comment
had to plunge on
power proved misapplied
waving her arms sideways

dreamed of eating ice
hung way off there
born with philosophy
they feel seems natural

ritual they had practised
for infinite energy
established comprehension
would have been the same

a cloud every night
become mere lucidity
bulging out of his head
upon her caked lips

EMPTILY

they bounce back from the screen
clean and ready
making parts of the body
an aesthetic obligation
before the skeleton bursts out

big snakes and small
might ask exactly what
a curve being any
point of view too there was something strange
see strange

winds
to conflicting effects

on the whole once knowledge is public

means non-speaking
it contained or required
unique because it is
a sudden crystallization of
garden

world
flatten out the paper

scales were finally overbalanced

to refrain from
association of
external perception
with a higher level of discard
sentence

was
the whole inward aspect

within the bounds of pure intention

could fold into
the quiet dirty pavement
within hardly an hour
on account of this photograph which
occurred

made
as stiffly dry as those

leaves turning up their pale undersides

stuck on the brim
two cheeks of a mandrill
prevent authority
fiery above the sullen wavelets
relief

point
angels and pins revel

merge together in a conception

scope to arrange
effect and appearance
a gap to fill after
the problem of lifting a canoe
designed

plain
but steel will rust observed

utilitarian energy

was little more
natural history
socially structured space
established a taxonomy based
behind

work
sudden eruption in

a landscape without time monuments

conventional
evading that pressure
lightly bound and fully
submerged and then rising out awe-struck
present

must
recall that things became

soft and sweet about the air speech moved

back to the couch
muffled by bad weather
he acted like something
leaving swirls of gas fumes in the air
sideways

long
though she lacked enough strength

supported by two square concrete posts

largest body
announced the pestilence
as currency to pay
self-replication efficiently
survived

stiff
with a few adjustments

about the nature of confusion

magnificent

islands and newly found

spectacular features

fatal secondary infections

over

hands

hot and moist often

before we consider that least glance

a world in which

naturally kept within

may have been even more

navigator to practice its skills

clearing

seams

similar in the mass

probably would not be credited

abilities
fallback position is
history of science
specialised cortical areas
without

more
variability

machinery for the basic throws

skimmed poor people
such specimens were all
especially the children
along a terminally depressed
board game

room
a strong defense posture

driving along a wilderness road

increasingly
weather when the city
was regarded as a
contradiction between the study
of a

new
kind of longing and that

of a responsive congregation

armies had swept
turned south and walked into
contempt because they were
unending supplies of substantial
stomachs

coarse
under rare directions

as easily deposed as climate

definition
pre-occupying time
with an express intent
to anchor scientific discourse
picture

meant
by a signal depends

stored in the dominant hemisphere

crops driven mad
late in their history
first approached the region
overwhelmingly greater than seed
can learn

raged
massive beyond the edge

into a device for producing

71

but out of this
higher mental command
proved in many respects
to be a physical distinction
nothing

plays
in freezing rain all night

towards the source of the stimulus

expresses an
attempt at another
new vision marking out
through periods of especial stress
common

in
clear traces of almost

adaptation to the emotion

colours can use

an existing building

years of the century

as a distinct body of grouping

money

proof

and the four elements

establish new subject positions

our sister in space

a designer award

must reflect back across

a grid where the barrier was moved

even

help

an everyday concept

the beaten have little to bargain

in appearance
frozen magnetism
no longer something
preoccupied with a need to cry
outside

set
immobile by question

subject to fits of rage and pity

an actress stares
objectively to see
to watch those objects change
coincidentally courageous
motor

mass
revising every dream

look with wonder at the stars and moon

material things
felt to be fanciful
fortune begins to fail
becomes a method of describing
creatures

scale
delicately coloured

creates a technology of space

universal
available surplus
during the modern age
not too bright or the images placed
dissolve

world
constructing a table

for accumulated collections

necessity
is in them less dispersed
she turned off the water
dismissing it from her mind with ease
suppressed

flow
not yet completely dark

forced him to show something of his hand

hooked up to sound
individually
firing long-range missiles
surprisingly large numbers of white
neon

strips
some plastic creatures

fending off enthusiastic crowds

improbably
suspended in the air
special scraps of paper
restricted access to the water
broken

weight
bringing a harsh glitter

still has no emotional meaning

illustrated
light gutters in the past
illuminating time
depending on the length of tubing
flame sound

shakes
into two equal parts

convertible one to the other

bursting into
all kinds of illicit
business undetected
regions would be affected whether
or not

since
such concern about stock

was white and was in a plastic bag

buttons and combs
a few hours before dark
will permit the export
of barbecued meat on long skewers
outstretched

crust
the clearing starts again

wiped out of a large part of their range

gaining daily
about its extension
the wheel has right-of-way
a dazzling samba around the ball
trembling

miss
no-one is looking back

society level at zero

DEFECTIVE DEFINITIONS

behind massive fortifications
click on the icon
venus enters your sign
where noise is a nuisance

your new finished hairline
going directly to the mouth
primarily restored fish
mad'a'fact video twice picked up

disorderly or funny
shape had a different birth
it becomes a food warmer
steaming clones par-boiled

able to scan reminder notes
break lends extra information
your computer can translate
dancing go full blast

head out for loading
exciting new realities
only when you get closer
the topic turns to planned

under hanging olives
totally blank stretches
a rush to passive investing
analysis worthless to discuss

how are we to find coffee?
fond fish? a high profile trap
not because of thrusting organisms
purely spends to get there

THE MOSQUITO AND THE MOON

it is hard enough
not merely a matter of belief
noise is another problem
continuing yet to confine
the great heap of spoils
turn left through the shop
something wrong, miscalculated
breaking cells completely
measuring is an aspect
surviving to produce
ending on a defined route
arranged in a ring
small localised holes
of intellectual depth
heavily coloured by allusions
brought the car to the kerb
speaking across a threshhold
charcoal marks indicate
towards the front of the bed
tragic but still breathing
they carry the old
letters running through decades
find emotional experience
filled with words
bearers of randomness
bumping and pushing
intimately familiar signs
not revealing location
milling images hard to retain
these were soldiers and sailors

restless edges of vibration
forced into twisted positions
another moment somewhere
mingled on the drawn curtain
grace caught unaware
awake with phantoms
made, used on the spot
the group shared in
techniques later refined
as they expanded eastward
off to an early start
plant materials were common
tightly bound on both sides
embedded in the landscape
an arc of stones
crudely made tools
eventually caught on
a gradient of sugar
persistently firing
in the brain and bloodstream
for oneself is not enough
the song once heard
inscribed in molecular processes
evoked to endure this
through the dark side
up out of chaos
slightly curved sound drops
from axis to circumference
keyed on the echo
a burglar alarm system

determines who a victim saw
doors eyes
shut before he turns
to sign in the body
being treated like a patient
examined in a good light
his face destroyed by shock
bars go full tilt
inside the ring move
communication options and emotions
a new atmosphere in matter
already underfinanced
wind and rain just
beginning to emerge
some senses work on
the power of the camera
measured by studying
modified to include isolation
to enter the dark compartment
reasonably clearly mapped
is to assume directive force
each time we remember
habits and seasons
change their properties
see wild animals
killed then tested
concentrate migrate
over a series of struts
between banks and islands
being the thin air

aware of existing devices
using solar energy
in the design of complex objects
not so ubiquitous as now
when the air is colder
an array of detectors
about low speed situations
learns the nature of life
perhaps fluids, hardware
systems that move people rapidly
die smashed into it
tightly coupled with growth
unavoidable delay
adapted the horse
in the humanities
expected ways fail
between signal and space
over heavily populated areas
a simple visual act
historically ephemeral
haunting without knowing
the perceptual grasp
of an adequate philosophy
natural images which seem
clear at the outset
accepted as a normal
stage of organization
of the actions of spirit
often thrust doubtless
towards an ideal of knowledge

continually threatening
the notion of large scale
hold an emotion
appropriate to grandeur
brought into contact
with things
brand new and never washed
broken wings
covered with burnt signs
ring the top edge
of whatever the dancer is doing
local colour
an abrupt radiance
to watch for in the city
makes your eyes jump
past tattoos of fake brick
rusty armoured space
nothing more modern
glowing coils of virus
cracks in their glaze
a halo slipped
folded to her throat
against the impossible air
where old things came from

NAME UNKNOWN

bare space
with neither flower nor picture
sunlight glows
through a half-empty peanut butter jar
the mixture cools
into the room's reality
gravediggers' increased productivity
may not be good for all
independent of measuring devices
monoliths eventually topple
across a system
of crystalline forms
a cat blinks
in the dust of a passing bus

under headlines
managed by the presenter
outer armour
produced in darkness fades
a thin supercold atmosphere
separates metal from its ores
gradually the soil becomes infertile
its fictional world explained or defined
to show measurable changes
combined with something outside themselves
still energetic enough
ancillary backgrounds throng
for only in a vacuum
does light invariably win

also the use of an image
must go into the open
of silent films
buttoned tight to keep
the secret of his alter ego
carefully patted into shape
in the twilight
concealed wires play
moving slightly in the breeze
whose slanting motion tracks
his head made of rubber
hung on the branch of a tree
smiling down upon the scene
unfolding towards the west

yet to be born at the moment
untroubled with systematic speculation
constructing optical instruments
to see things close up
the road is open leading
to a sense of volume
rich yet sparsely defined
always growing and deviating
towards primary colours
conscious of intensification
in the narrow corridors of the modern
this direction
will have time to name itself
marked with a drip of wax

in that logical order
bizarre scandals precipitate
about his greatest interests
farewell to the beach
bright waterlilies sagging
perhaps ruined by jealousy
more a complex work of art
announcing to the world
various causes of ideas
unsung by constant nagging
gradually she calms down
to salvage from the fire
vitality overcome by emotion
converging on catastrophe

a sense of being deserted
emerging to be good
on their shoulders
scattered throughout spacious
influence reveals their pathetic
character measured against
external wooden fire escapes
a neurosis about ability
run to be discarded
before curtain time
too many facts
assume a parody of none
substituted for the original
by fertility of imagination

somehow admitted from the shadows
echoing eyes pierce
the defence of compassion
as a musical instrument
among genuine monsters
purifies awareness
into a tranquil habit
to spoil his fine work
condition is imperceptive
hope for an elegant event
slow to understand
the surface should be loose
a pastel colour plan
cropped through the seasons

tear away whole sections
of what is good
bags of camel's hair
a blue that carries further
the unlikeness of dusk and chaos
crossing a stream
where tributaries enter a river
you can't wait for science
to drain that space of wet earth dry
the face seems to lack contour
nothing is left but a vast expanse
deep grooves of habit
trodden into the soil
under a full moon crossed by a vulture

exhausted by their experiences
his body spreads
disease rumour spiced
with a touch of grace
a crackle of wood burning
sweeps the whole scene
getting dark in the east
where no sound enters
notice the wires are pulled
by no splendour, imagery or power
vision does more than see
the habit of infinite parenthesis
changes of fashion stumbling
forever over the plains of time

MUTED HAWKS

intense physical conflict
confuses the two areas
renders capital concrete
which annoys the generals
paid by the citizen

formalised heaven not unlike
reason you must operate
in our imaginations
to act except in ignorance
sinister rather than admirable

abrupt illumination
while he stared at his cage
the day slipped by
retaining knowledge
in a declining body

to its logical conclusion
in a way no civilisation
represented as natural
or advancing the public good
should have given early warning

comes comfort which in turn
poking its reflecting eye
up from within
has always been for hire
open to exploitation by experts

through these great rooms
abstract structures dominate
being perfect imitations
perhaps for future use
beneath their dignity to run

hearings to overhang an area
obviously ridiculous
resemble parody
more consciously integrated
on interests of the regime

brilliance an inherited machine
capable of unlearning
what would have to change
beneath the patina
of interest and doubt

become a major barrier
so strategically important
followed by collapse
painted in great detail
to resemble opera

to eliminate war
airs of evenings impinge
the place or date of origin
blocking the critical path
only able to be rent

no pattern from them
dark indeed came quickly
memories of it vague
time had become leather
regrettably informal

transformations into dogs
ransom or rescue
smaller food animals
when human figures occur
antennae rising from their heads

WIT WITHER

"Such joy . . . . such desperate joy!" (Willem de Kooning)

two major patterns
produced a realist view
any thing may be an instance
substantiated by observing
the primary direction of dream
no matter how specific
the way in which space
would change or distort
boundaries more precise
despite more flexible distance
to accommodate need
unpacking symbols
in control of all situations
the currents
justifying selection
baking bread and drawing water
introduce us to context
a carefully posed photograph
juxtaposing monuments
begging with black slogans
which we cannot imagine
out of a fashion parade
actions will be understood
detected outside
those same skills
open for others
demonstrate that muscles
have burned away

from obscure lines
images not alive
still not exactly dead
at the centre of reflection
of the electronic world
feel details about
the inside of each
nature of the event
command our attention
inspiration of smoke
mostly drugs
his mental efforts
between sisters
entering thick lovers
hands-on
a glimpse of other eras
mainly marks on the dial
daily passes
work their replacing
down routine firings
poised ambitious to provide
conscious literary originals
happen may even think
know or other cues
required in your unit
scrabbling at the prospect
while you need
storming with
affiliate that produces
shaped bright overflow

in the complete
museum dedicated to
former documenting
penguins, sea lions
carefully singing magic
locked in on her
stripped out
arms folded
odour of decaying
interest and concentration
passing under columns
of white stones
on a chrome
motor whirr
inched along enticement
past spiderwebs
under his arms
turned squarely on
instinctive impulse
deeper into dereliction
beneath irregular
heat inside
consideration of delusion
a place to crawl to
and endlessly loop
among the folds of garments

ERRORY

joined harmonizing the best
so it needn't wait
phrase: the question are you sure?
hanging three feet off the ground
silent, absolutely quiet
headquarters — we travelled north
clawing back small shelter
hung with screaming
on the same rig
blended in enthusiasm
as the race approached
through cracks in snow
free-falling into mind
alive with brightness shivering
instantly into sleep
changed, re-formed
they run, they run
with madness into chutes
of changed values
all of them conventional
vibrations of division
dare to refuse the glass
lazily through long green
discrete landing sites
to a transmitting unit
over the protective line
wave patterns in space
form black against
sifted patches of moonlight
birds move in the dark

their faint contours
singing small notes
to the rhythm of a train
so empty at this hour
silence in between
contains the words
things whizz past
once more
the sound of calculation
by indirect means
receives its full due
along the wet pavement
human flesh
fallen in all directions
to fresh eyes
something to do with the sky
senselessly dishevelled
resolves and fixes
the foundation
desirable to guard against
relative soundness of approach
including human shapes
used by the dealer
connecting them
to a sense of common
unforeseeable properties of relics
considered in place
so deceptive
their firesides play
optimism for its object

without arousing
constitutional tradition
beyond the rules of the game
hailstones imagine
moist sea air
disordered beyond it rise
drearier philosophies
to resist retrogression
faster than anything
directly stimulating receptors
attention moves
many possible representations
inside the heart
decayed into blackness
fine details of the scene
creep along for years
hard to become
immune to a predator
silhouettes of participants
dangle in their own data
faint green clouds
in almost pure alcohol
calibrate the equipment
to assume a more personal form
susceptible to psychic influences
does not contempt breed
often in disguise?
slipping past a window
on communal stairs
into faded yellow

flashed with orange
slanting through smoke
swished into a perfect dome
dissatisfied when calm returns
centered around a food animal
mastery of areas
managed to neutralize
subjects into waves
to destroy commmunication
more easily on scanty pasture

DARK SENSES

bones show through images
of friends though they
still move in dialogue
in darkness what relief

forgive me, it's a dream
standing alone, waving
in search of its lost era
not just geography

walking parallel streets
of tropical flames
with a political broom
ominous as a smoke signal

over a farewell meal
of dust in the dust
before an open window
weather permitting

step sharply within
the labyrinth of raw meat
jingling those keys
dimmed by sweat

unthinking insects click, rustle
for bare subsistence
in the skeletons of organisations
inexorably crushed by vice

they themselves go into hiding
one on top of another
in their natural colours
green smocks, masks and goggles

taking likenesses
to build a screen
alongside the trail
of pearl lightbulb shards

this curiously shaped barrier
contains gestures and rites
simulated leopard skins
smart cards and our ideas

for fear of disturbing
the pose of philosophy
fashionable at the time
they stand in complete silence

in unbroken sunlight
wearing masks
as aids to memory
attributed to interiors unknown

they did not break
under their own weight
the experience of generations
proved far more effective

acts of representation respond
in order to survive desire
cheated by false hopes
in voices hardly above a whisper

local weather prophets
proclaim their laws of storm
radioactive rain restricted
to areas over toxic waste

the nightmare atmosphere of ruin
washes away in close-up
striking spatial effects predicted
if the mask is joyful

produce a sublime gesture
opposed to voice or action
a system of reflections ordering
the necessity of ornament

OUT OF A SUDDEN

(Riva san Vitale, August 30th 1995)

the alphabet wonders
what it should do
paper feels useless
colours lose hue

while all musical notes
perform only in blue

a lombardy poplar
shadows the ground
drifted with swansdown
muffling the sound

at the tip of the lake
of the road to the south

above in the night sky
scattered by chance
stars cease their motion
poppies don't dance

in the grass standing still
by the path no-one walks

ROOF BOOKS
Partial List

Andrews, Bruce. **EX WHY ZEE.** 112p. $10.95.
Andrews, Bruce. **Getting Ready To Have Been Frightened**. 116p. $7.50.
Benson, Steve. **Blue Book**. Copub. with The Figures. 250p. $12.50
Bernstein, Charles. **Islets/Irritations**. 112p. $9.95.
Bernstein, Charles (editor). **The Politics of Poetic Form**. 246p. $12.95; cloth $21.95.
Brossard, Nicole. **Picture Theory**. 188p. $11.95.
Davies, Alan. **Active 24 Hours**. 100p. $5.
Davies, Alan. **Signage**. 184p. $11.
Davies, Alan. **Rave**. 64p. $7.95.
Day, Jean. **A Young Recruit**. 58p. $6.
Di Palma, Ray. **Motion of the Cypher**. 112p. $10.95.
Di Palma, Ray. **Raik**. 100p. $9.95.
Doris, Stacy. **Kildare**. 104p. $9.95
Dreyer, Lynne. **The White Museum**. 80p. $6.
Edwards, Ken. **Good Science.** 80p. $9.95.
Eigner, Larry. **Areas Lights Heights**. 182p. $12, $22 (cloth).
Gizzi, Michael. **Continental Harmonies**. 92p. $8.95.
Gottlieb, Michael. **Ninety-Six Tears**. 88p. $5.
Grenier, Robert. **A Day at the Beach**. 80p. $6.
Hills, Henry. **Making Money**. 72p. $7.50. VHS videotape $24.95. Book & tape $29.95.
Hunt, Erica. **Local History**. 80 p. $9.95.
Inman, P. **Criss Cross**. 64 p. $7.95.
Inman, P. **Red Shift**. 64p. $6.
Lazer, Hank. **Doublespace**. 192 p. $12.
Mac Low, Jackson. **Representative Works: 1938–1985**. 360p. $12.95, $18.95 (cloth).
Mac Low, Jackson. **Twenties**. 112p. $8.95.
Moriarty, Laura. **Rondeaux**. 107p. $8.
Neilson, Melanie. **Civil Noir**. 96p. $8.95.
Pearson, Ted. **Planetary Gear**. 72p. $8.95.
Perelman, Bob. **Virtual Reality**. 80p. $9.95.
Piombino, Nick, **The Boundary of Blur**. 128p. $13.95
Robinson, Kit. **Balance Sheet.** 112 p. $9.95.
Robinson, Kit. **Ice Cubes**. 96p. $6.
Scalapino, Leslie. **Objects in the Terrifying Tense Longing from Taking Place.** 88p. $9.95.
Seaton, Peter. **The Son Master**. 64p. $5.
Sherry, James. **Popular Fiction**. 84p. $6.
Silliman, Ron. **The New Sentence**. 200p. $10.
Silliman, Ron. **N/O**. 112 p. $10.95.
Templeton, Fiona. **YOU—The City**. 150p. $11.95.
Ward, Diane. **Human Ceiling**. 80p. $8.95.
Ward, Diane. **Relation**. 64p. $7.50.
Watten, Barrett. **Progress**. 122p. $7.50.

Discounts (same title): 1 – 4 books—20%; 5 or more—40%. (Postage 4th Class incl., UPS extra)
For complete list or ordering, send check or money order in U.S. dollars to:
SEGUE FOUNDATION, 303 East 8th Street, New York, NY 10009